TABLE OF CONTENTS

Formation of Fossils	1*
Formation of Fossils	1a
Geological Time Scale - I	2*
Geological Time Scale - I	2a
Geological Time Scale - II	3*
Geological Time Scale - II	3a
Geological Events - Timeline	3b
Paleozoic Era - I	4*
Paleozoic Era - I	4a
Paleozoic Era - II	5*
Paleozoic Era - II	5a
Carboniferous Swamp	6*
Carboniferous Swamp	6a
Mesozoic Era - *Triassic period*	7*
Mesozoic Era - *Triassic period*	7a
Mesozoic Era - *Family Tree of the Dinosaurs*	7b
Mesozoic Era - *Jurassic period*	8*
Mesozoic Era - *Jurassic period*	8a
Mesozoic Era - *Jurassic period*	8b
Mesozoic Era - *Cretaceous period*	9*
Mesozoic Era - *Cretaceous period*	9a
Mesozoic Era - *Cretaceous period*	9b
Cenozoic Era - *Tertiary period*	10*
Cenozoic Era - *Tertiary period*	10a
Cenozoic Era - *Quaternary period*	11*
Cenozoic Era - *Quaternary period*	11a
Prehistoric People	12*
Prehistoric People	12a

For final testing and review:

A Last Look - Part I	I
A Last Look - Part II	II
A Last Look - Part III	III
A Last Look - Part IV	IV

* Full-color transparencies are found at the back of the book. Each transparency should be used to introduce the corresponding unit.

TEACHING GUIDE

Page 1 FORMATION OF FOSSILS

CONCEPT: Fossils, formed in three basic ways, are evidence of ancient life.

BACKGROUND INFORMATION: Fossils are any evidence, such as remains, impressions, or traces of organisms, of a former geological age. Not only are fossils clues to ancient organisms, but also to the climatic and topographical conditions of past times. Most fossils were formed in water. Plant and animal remains under water are not as rapidly decomposed as remains on land. Fossils were formed in three basic ways: 1) The actual remains were preserved, i.e., insects that were trapped in resinous secretions of ancient trees, which later hardened to amber; and mammoths discovered in the perpetually frozen subsoil of Siberia and Alaska. 2) All of the original substance dissolves away but an impression remains, i.e., a shelled creature buried in ancient sediments left an external form of itself, called a mold, when the shell material dissolved. The cavity left by the dissolved shell may have become filled with sediment, forming a cast. 3) Organic matter is replaced, atom by atom, by mineral matter, i.e., petrified wood is the result of wood material having been replaced by silica preserving the minutest details. Bones may have had their pores filled with mineral substances and thus remained substantially unaltered.

ENRICHMENT ACTIVITIES: 1. Find out about the fossils from the La Brea Tar Pits in California and fossils found in the Grand Canyon. 2. Find out about the work of the British geologists James Hutton, William Smith, and Charles Lyell.

ANSWER KEY:
Page 1 1. Preservation of actual remains; molds, casts, and imprints; replacement by mineral matter 2. marine life, such as shells and trilobites **Study Question:** Soft coal fields had an abundance of plants and trees buried in swampy land under layers of sediment, and because of great heat and pressure, some of the original plant material can still be found as fossils in the coal.
Page 1a 1. A. Preservation of actual remains B. Molds, casts, and imprints C. Replacement by mineral matter 2. 1. amber 2. tar pit 3. fern leaf 4. dinosaur footprints 5. trilobite 6. petrified wood 7. vertebra 3. a. 2 b. 1 c. 1 d. 3 e. 2

Page 2 GEOLOGICAL TIME SCALE - I

CONCEPTS: 1. Geological evidence indicates the beginning of life took place on the earth approximately 2.5 billion years ago. 2. The fossil record shows that the earliest forms of life were marine organisms.

BACKGROUND INFORMATION: The geological history of life from the Pre-Cambrian Era is meager. There are indications that life was somewhat abundant; the fossil remains, however, are limited. Some of the most ancient fossils found are those of simple, aquatic plants. The calcareous algae were microscopic in size. They grew in colonies and large globular masses of limestone. Paleobotanists have found microscopic fossils which resemble bacteria or simple fungi in chert. The fossil remains of the Paleozoic are very abundant from the Cambrian period on. It is believed that all animal life was invertebrate and marine. Most common fossils are the trilobite and brachiopod. In the Ordovician period the cephalopods became the rulers of the sea. The first vertebrate, a primitive fish, also came into existence during this period. During the Silurian period the corals had their beginnings and the crinoids became very abundant. The first land invertebrate, a scorpion-like creature, appeared, as did millipedes. The Devonian period is marked by a diversity of fauna and flora. This period is often referred to as the "Age of Fishes" due to the extreme abundance of fish in the seas. Sharks and lungfish developed, and from the lungfish evolved the primitive amphibians. The first land plants appeared. Many of the plants first inhabited swamps and low, wet regions in river valleys. Invertebrate land life also rapidly developed - spiders and land snails. The Mississippian and Pennsylvanian periods are often called collectively the Carboniferous period because of the predominance of coal-forming swamps. The Mississippian swampy conditions favored the development of the amphibians. The Pennsylvanian period was much like the Mississippian. However, it is marked by the greater development of land organisms. During the Permian period geological changes caused the elimination of many swamps and of shallow marine waters. The reptiles diversified and became the main land vertebrates. Some modern forms of insects developed.

ENRICHMENT ACTIVITIES: 1. Research information about Pre-Cambrian jellyfish and worm fossils. 2. Find out what kind of Paleozoic fossils are found in the area near your home.

ANSWER KEY:
Page 2 1. marine waters 2. during the Devonian period **Study Question:** 1. Most organisms were soft-bodied and did not form fossils well; also, most of the rocks were of igneous and metamorphic nature and fossils are not formed in such rocks.
Page 2a 1. See transparency 2 for names of eras and periods 2. a. 500,000,000 - 570,000,000 years ago b. 570,000,000 - 4,500,000,000 years ago

c. 400,000,000 - 430,000,000 years ago d. 280,000,000 - 310,000,000 years ago e. 430,000,000 - 500,000,000 years ago 3. a. Devonian b. Pennsylvanian c. Silurian d. Ordovician e. Mississippian/Pennsylvanian

Page 3 GEOLOGICAL TIME SCALE - II

CONCEPTS: The Mesozoic Era was a time of dramatic development of living things. 2. The development of the human species is a relatively recent event in geologic history.

BACKGROUND INFORMATION: The Mesozoic Era is often referred to as the "Age of Reptiles" or "Age of the Dinosaurs." The reptiles were very abundant and became the dominant land vertebrates. They exhibited a great diversity of form from small chicken-sized creatures to huge beasts like the Brontosaurus. The dinosaurs inhabited both the land and seas, and some forms developed into flying creatures. Among the various dinosaurs were carnivores and herbivores. Early in the Mesozoic Era the conifers had their origin. The petrified forests of Arizona give evidence of the large size of these early conifers. Plant life was abundant and widespread, possibly due to the warm climate. During the Cretaceous period the hardwood trees developed, as did the flowering plants. The mammals made a modest beginning in the Triassic period. The birds evolved later in the Jurassic period. It was also during the Jurassic period that most of the modern forms of insects appeared. Early in the Cenozoic Era the dinosaurs became extinct, possibly due to climatic changes and the egg-eating habits of the early mammals. The mammals then became the main vertebrates. The flowering plants became established as the main land plants. Prairies of grasses, including the grains, developed. It is thought that perhaps sometime during the Pliocene epoch prehistoric humans evolved. The early Quaternary period was marked by the development of modern mammals and man.

ENRICHMENT ACTIVITIES: 1. Research the origin of the names of the periods in the Mesozoic Era. 2. Find out what effect glaciation in the Pleistocene epoch had on living things in North America.

ANSWER KEY:
Page 3 1. Mesozoic 2. Quaternary **Study Question:** The scales on the legs, similar eggs, and an egg tooth at hatching.
Page 3a 1. See transparency 3 for names of eras and periods. 2. a. Triassic b. Tertiary c. Cretaceous d. Jurassic e. Cretaceous f. Quaternary 3. a. 2,000,000 to 65,000,000 years ago b. 65,000,000 to 135,000,000 years ago c. 180,000,000 to 230,000,000 years ago d. 135,000,000 to 180,000,000 years ago
Page 3b 1. Appalachian Mts. 2. Pennsylvanian 3. Pre-Cambrian 4. Tertiary 5. Cambrian and Mississippian

Page 4 PALEOZOIC ERA - I

CONCEPT: The early periods of the Paleozoic Era are noted for their diverse, invertebrate fauna; aquatic forms evolved into terrestrial forms during this era.

BACKGROUND INFORMATION: Ancient life on earth was marine. The warm, shallow seas teamed with invertebrate fauna which had rigid parts or shell structures. These shell-forming organisms have left an abundant fossil record. Shells of brachiopods were in abundance on the ocean shores during the early periods of the Paleozoic Era. Brachiopods have two shells (valves), unequal in size. The adult form attached itself to submerged objects and fed on organic matter strained from the water. Trilobites were also abundant. These arthropods had a three-segmented body with many legs, enabling it to crawl on the sea bottom and up onto wet, sandy beaches. Corals of the solitary and colonial types came into existence in the Silurian period. Crinoids, a plant-like looking animal, appeared during the Ordovician period. This "sea-lily" looking animal had a supporting column (stem), a "flower-head" holding the creature's vital organs, and feathery arms which served to gather food. A shelled animal, the cephalopod, which evolved in the Ordovician period, was the ancestor of modern forms: squid, octopus, and cuttlefish. Ancient cephalopods had a tapering shell with tentacles protruding from the opening. This mollusk became very abundant, with some species reaching a length of 4.5m. The first fishes appeared in early Paleozoic times. They were small in size and possessed heavy dermal armor of bony plates. The early amphibians made their appearance during the Devonian period. These creatures had long bodies with short, stubby legs and long tails. These were the first vertebrates to leave the water and take up a more or less permanent residence on land. While animal life in early Paleozoic times was becoming diverse and abundant, plant life was also developing. Primitive land plants were widespread during the Devonian period.

ENRICHMENT ACTIVITIES: 1. Find out about the various types of primitive fishes such as crossopterygians and the lungfish. 2. Find out how salt deposits were formed during the Silurian period.

ANSWER KEY:
Page 4 1. trilobites, brachiopods, corals, cephalopods, crinoids, primitive fish and amphibians, primitive land plants 2. warm, shallow waters **Study Question:** Trilobites — body depressed with three distinct parts: head, thorax, and tail; head and tail were covered, thorax was jointed; the entire body was longitudinally trilobed by a pair of grooves that separated a rounded, central axis from the lateral areas. Stegocephalians — heads were armored with dermal bones, giving the skull a massive, solid appearance; four-footed, long bodies and weak legs, looking somewhat like a modern "giant salamander."

Copyright © 1986 — Milliken Publishing Co. All rights reserved.   Fossils and Prehistoric Life

Page 4a 1. A. Cambrian B. Ordovician C. Silurian D. Devonian 2. E. trilobite F. brachiopod G. coral H. cephalopod I. crinoid 3. J. primitive fish K. primitive amphibian L. primitive land plant 4. a. 4,S b. 3,C c. 8,O d. 1,S e. 5,D f. 2,O g. 6,O h. 7,D

Page 5 PALEOZOIC ERA - II

CONCEPT: The Mississippian, Pennsylvanian, and Permian periods, the three latest periods of the Paleozoic Era, varied in duration and each had distinct natural occurrences.

BACKGROUND INFORMATION: During the Mississippian period, most of the Mississippi Valley was covered by water, causing warm swamplands supporting different forms of life — plant, insect, and amphibian. These life forms flourished. Among the invertebrates of the Mississippian period were crinoids, blastoids, spiny brachiopods, and ammonites. The corkscrew and lace-type bryozoa were distinctive life forms of this period. Sharks, known as shell crushers, were a distinct form of vertebrates. On land areas, there were thick swamp forests where many varieties of land plants thrived — scale trees, huge mosses and ferns, scouring rushes, and seed ferns. The Pennsylvanian period is known for its formation of vast coal deposits and a wide variety of animal life — centipedes, spiders, scorpions, snails, and primitive insects such as dragonflies and cockroaches. Both dragonflies and cockroaches were very large in size. During the Pennsylvanian period the first reptiles appeared. Evidence shows an abundance and variety of animals living on land during this period. Land would undergo a drastic change in the Permian period. There were alternating periods of heat and cold, humidity and aridity. Land upheavals, desert formation, and glaciation all had an effect on life forms of the Permian period. Many species of plant and animal life became extinct — carboniferous plants, trilobites, blastoids, and others. New plant species appeared (conebearers), marine animal species expanded (ammonoid cephalopods and gastropods), and amphibians and reptiles continued to flourish. Fin-back reptiles were common; early ancestors of mammals were present at this time. The end of the Permian period brought the Paleozoic Era to a close.

ENRICHMENT ACTIVITIES: 1. Find out about the formation of the Appalachian Mountains and the Grand Canyon. 2. Find out about the Great Ice Age affecting South America, South Africa, India, and Australia.

ANSWER KEY:
Page 5 1. bryozoa, primitive arthropods, Lepidodendrons, Dimetrodons, sharks 2. Cockroaches 3-4 inches long were common. The scale trees had close-set leaves that left permanent leaf scars on the trunk and limbs. These scars made them appear scaled. Fossils of these trees are often mistaken for petrified snake skins. **Study Question:** Species of "coal-producing plants" - scale trees, huge mosses and ferns, scouring rushes, and seed ferns thrived and flourished in the thick swamp-forests of the Mississippian and Pennsylvanian periods. During thes two periods vast coal fields were formed and are referred to as the Carboniferous periods.
Page 5a 1. A. Mississippian B. Pennsylvanian C. Permian 2. E. Lepidodendron or scale tree 3. D. bryozoa F. primitive arthropod G. Dimetrodon H. shark 4. a. 4-Pa. b. 5-Per. c. 2-Per. d. 1-M. e. 3-Pa. f. 1-M. g. 3-Pa.

Page 6 CARBONIFEROUS SWAMP

CONCEPTS: 1. The Mississippian and Pennsylvanian periods are often referred to as the Carboniferous period. 2. Vast swamps and amphibians are characteristic of these periods.

BACKGROUND INFORMATION: During the Mississippian period the world climate was generally warm with heavy rainfall. There were large areas of lowlands covered with shallow water. These swamps supported luxuriant vegetation. The tree ferns resembled some of our modern forest-floor ferns. The primitive ferns had huge fronds, however, and some grew to a height of 10 meters. One of the most abundant species of plants was the scale tree. These specimens were giant plants. Some were 30 meters tall and had base diameters of nearly 1.5 meters. The scale-like leaves of the scale tree grew directly from the trunk and the branches. The leaves were shed throughout the year, leaving distinct leaf scars. Large numbers of giant rushes grew in Pennsylvanian swamps. These rushes were structurally identical to the horsetail rushes of today except for their very large size. The cordaites were ancestors of our modern gymnosperms, the conifers. They grew to a height of 15 meters. The carboniferous swamps were the habitats of the primitive amphibians and insects. During this period the seas invaded the swamps periodically. The submerged vegetation formed massive layers of debris. During the later portion of the period, the climate became cooler and the vast swamps declined. The plant material became compressed when it was buried under layers of sediment. Slowly the organic material was converted to coal. It has been estimated that about twenty feet of uncompressed vegetative debris was required to form one foot of bituminous coal. In some of the coal fields there are beds more than sixty-feet thick, giving evidence of the luxuriance of these ancient swamplands.

ENRICHMENT ACTIVITIES: 1. Research the plant fossils found in coal balls and studied by the peel technique. 2. Find out about the peat, bituminous, and anthracite coal deposits in North America.

ANSWER KEY:
Page 6 1. A lowland area with shallow swamps supporting luxuriant vegetation 2. Amphibians **Study Question:** Plant material was compressed under layers of sediments. The carbon material remained and formed a black rock.
Page 6a 1. A. scale tree B. giant dragonfly C. lungfish D. cockroach E. primitive amphibian F. tree fern 2. Answers may vary. There were no hardwood trees. 3. their large size 4. warm and humid 5. The climate became cooler; the uplift of land caused the disappearance of swampy areas.

Page 7 MESOZOIC ERA *Triassic Period*

CONCEPTS: 1. The Triassic period marks the beginning of the "Age of the Reptiles." 2. Many new kinds of invertebrates and plants appeared.

BACKGROUND INFORMATION: The first period of the Mesozoic Era is the Triassic period. It began about 230,000,000 years ago and lasted about 50,000,000 years. Plant and animal life differed from the preceding Paleozoic periods. Dominant examples of plant life in the Triassic period were the conifers, broadleaf ferns, and cycads. Examples of common marine invertebrates were gastropods, pelecypods, crustacea, and ammonites. Reef-building corals were starting to form present-day coral reefs throughout the world. Sharks and bony fishes were common in marine areas; reptiles were fast becoming the dominant form of life among the vertebrates. Phytosaurs, semiaquatic animals resembling crocodiles, were very common. Early dinosaurs were small during this period, compared to the "giants" of later periods. Triassic dinosaurs were slender of build, and few species reached a length of more than 6 meters. Most were bipedal and shaped like a kangaroo, with powerful hind legs and a thick powerful tail used for balancing. It is believed that these dinosaurs ran like an ostrich rather than leaping about. One of the largest dinosaurs of this period, Plateosaurus, was about 6 meters long; one of the smallest dinosaurs, Podokesaurus, was about 1 meter long. An early mammal-like reptile of the Triassic period was the Cynognathus. Fossil remains of this animal, chiefly teeth and jaw fragments, provide evidence of distinct mammalian characteristics.

ENRICHMENT ACTIVITIES: 1. Research the reptiles that dominated the seas and oceans. 2. Find out about theories that indicate some dinosaurs were warm-blooded.

ANSWER KEY:
Page 7. 1. Plateosaurus and Podokesaurus 2. conifer **Study Question:** snails, clams, lobster-like crustaceans, and corals
Page 7a 1. A. conifer B. Cynognathus C. Placodus D. Phytosaurus E. Plateosaurus F. Podokesaurus G. broadleaf fern 2. Phytosaurus 3. Cynognathus 4. Placodus 5. Podokesaurus, Plateosaurus
Page 7b 1. Therapsida 2. Triassic 3. Saurischia 4. Jurassic 5. Anklosaurus 6. Thecodontia

Page 8 - MESOZOIC ERA *Jurassic Period*

CONCEPT: Plant and animal life flourished during the Jurassic period; noteworthy were the unusual reptiles called dinosaurs.

BACKGROUND INFORMATION: Climate during the Jurassic period appeared to have been mild throughout the world, except for a few hot, dry desert-like areas. Plant life — (pines, conifers, ginkos, scouring rushes, and cycads) flourished in the lush forests. Cycads were so abundant that this period is often called the "Age of Cycads." Animal life - (flies, dragonflies, beetles, grasshoppers, cockroaches, termites, mites, butterflies) was abundant. A distinct "trademark" of the Jurassic period was the growth and development of reptiles, especially the dinosaurs. It was in this period that the dinosaurs attained their greatest size; some were nearly 20 meters long. Some of the dominant dinosaurs of this period were the Diplodocus, Stegosaurus, and Brontosaurus. The Stegosaurus had a double row of triangular bony plates that ran from its head to the end of its tail. It fought with its back to the enemy and defended itself with four large, sharp, bony spikes on its tail. The front of its jaw formed a sort of beak; it was a herbivorous reptile. Stegosaurus weighed about 10 tons, had a 2½ ounce brain, and ranged from 5.5m to 7m long. One of the largest and best known dinosaurs is the Brontosaurus or "Thunder Lizard." It weighed about 30 tons, had a brain weighing less than a pound, and was about 20m long. It had a very long, thin neck and tiny head, very thick legs, and a long tail. It walked on all four feet and was a herbivorous reptile. It was an amphibious reptile, living on land and in water. In the seas, the ichthyosaurs were at the peak of their development. These were long, fish-like reptiles about 3m long that used their feet and tails as paddles for swimming. During the Jurassic period the first flying reptiles, pterosaurs, appeared. "True birds," the Archaeopteryx, first appeared during this period, as well. Mammals also began to diversify during the Jurassic period.

ENRICHMENT ACTIVITIES: 1. Find out about other dinosaurs - Ornitholestes, Allosaurus, and Comptosaurus. 2. Find out about the fossil locality of Solenhofen, Bavaria.

ANSWER KEY:
Page 8 1. Stegosaurus — armored reptile, Ichthyosaurus — marine reptile, Brontosaurus — amphibious reptile, Cycad — palm-like seed plant 2. Stegosaurus — armored body with spiked tail, Ichthyosaurus — streamlined body for fast swimming and dolphin-like in appearance, Brontosaurus — large body, long thin neck and tiny head, very thick legs and long tail. **Study**

Question: pterodactyls — wingspread of about 1m; some had tails and some were tailless; had teeth and four legs and could walk on all four legs when on ground; wings were of skin stretched along the body between the hind limb and a very long fourth "little finger," leaving the other digits free to serve as claws; Plesiosaurus — had a broad, turtle-like body, long neck and long flippers; clumsy and slow, they paddled their way like marine turtles.

Page 8a 1. A. Jurassic 2. B. Stegosaurus C. Ichthyosaurus D. Brontosaurus E. Cycad 3. reptiles 4. 1. a 2. c 3. d 4. b 5. d 6. c 7. a 8. b

Page 8b 1. a, c, d, f, i, k 2. a, d, e, g, h, j, k 3. a. thunder reptile b. fish reptile c. terrible reptile d. wing finger e. almost reptile 4. a. Ichthyosaurus b. Archaeopteryx c. Pteranodon d. Stegosaurus

Page 9 - MESOZOIC ERA *Cretaceous Period*

CONCEPT: The Cretaceous period, marked by geologic unrest and the extinction of the dinosaur, is noted for the appearance of deciduous trees and flowering plants.

BACKGROUND INFORMATION: During the Cretaceous period, the dinosaurs had their climax. Perhaps one of the most awesome of the dinosaurs was the Tyrannosaurus. This huge reptile was nearly 16m long. Its long head (1.2m or 4 feet) was 6m (twenty feet) off the ground. Its mouth was filled with many teeth, some of which were six inches long. These teeth indicate that it was a carnivorous animal. The front feet were very small and perhaps used only for grasping. The hind legs, however, were very large and equipped with powerful claws. A heavily armored ground-dweller dinosaur was the Ankylosaurus. It had a fat body armed with lateral spines. The head was small, and the tail was a thick, spike-studded, club-like appendage. One of the largest flying reptiles was the Pteranodon. It had a wingspread of nearly 7.5m. The body was the size of a turkey and the head had a characteristic crest. These reptiles appeared to have spent much time soaring in the air over water since there is evidence of fish in their diet. The Cretaceous period ushered in the appearance of flowering plants and deciduous trees. The flora began to take on a modern aspect. Toward the end of this period, the climate began to change; it became cool. Desert areas and glaciers were formed in various places. There was great geologic unrest resulting in the formation of the Rocky Mountain chain and the Andes Mountain chain.

ENRICHMENT ACTIVITIES: 1. Find out about other Cretaceous reptiles such as Triceratops and the mosasaurs. 2. Find out about the formation of the Rocky Mountain chain.

ANSWER KEY:
Page 9 1. Reptiles - Pteranodon (flying), Tyrannosaurus (carnivorous), Ankylosaurus (heavily armored), flowering plants and deciduous trees 2. Pteranodon — flying reptile with huge wingspread; Tyrannosaurus — very large body, head and teeth, awesome in appearance, carnivorous; Ankylosaurus — heavily armored, ground dweller, herbivorous **Study Question:** Tiny brains and low intelligence were responsible for extinction; the disappearance of swamps and a change in plant life caused dinosaurs to starve to death; an abundance of mammals stole and ate dinosaur eggs, leading to dinosaur extinction; when climate changed from warm to very cold at the end of this period, dinosaurs could not adapt.

Page 9a 1. A. Cretaceous 2. B. Pteranodon C. flowering plants and deciduous trees D. Tyrannosaurus E. Ankylosaurus 3. Tyrannosaurus 4. 1. d 2. a 3. c 4. a 5. b 6. d 7. a 8. d

Page 9b 1. reptiles, claws, wings, teeth 2. 1. P 2. H 3. D 4. I 5. D 3. bones, feathers; eggs 4. 1. V 2. F 3. T

Page 10 CENOZOIC ERA *Tertiary Period*

CONCEPTS: 1. The Cenozoic Era is often called the "Age of the Mammals." 2. During the Tertiary period large numbers of modern plant and animal species developed.

BACKGROUND INFORMATION: The Tertiary period of this era, which began about 65,000,000 years ago and lasted about 63,000,000 years, is often divided into five epochs — Paleocene, the oldest epoch, Eocene, Oligocene, Miocene, and Pliocene. In the Paleocene epoch the marsupials, primates, insectivores, rodents, and carnivores appeared. The early marsupials were essentially like the opossum of today. The primates, such as the flying lemur, Planetetherium, were about as big as a squirrel. Insectivores were also very small. Mice, rats, and squirrels were common examples of rodents. The carnivores showed some specialization: sharp, shearing teeth, and sharp claws. Mammals of the Paleocene epoch were primitive and small. Eocene forms were somewhat larger. A large flightless bird of this epoch, Diatryma, was about 2 meters tall. It had a very stout neck and a head about as large as that of a horse. The animals of the Oligocene epoch took on an appearance somewhat like the animals of today. The large rhino-like animal of the Oligocene epoch, Brontotherium, stood about 3 meters tall at the shoulder. Increases in herds of grazing animals and the evolution of different species occurred in the Miocene because of climate changes (more arid) and the development of vast prairie lands. Early horses, Eohippus, now attained the size of small ponies. Pliocene animals were even more highly developed than those of early Tertiary epochs. Horses continued their evolution with the first single-toed horse, Pheohippus, making its appearance. Camels, rhinoceroses, and giant ground sloths, all true mastodons, and an early armadillo, Glyptodont, were common animals of this epoch. During the Pliocene epoch, fossil remains indicate the existence of early human-like apes.

ENRICHMENT ACTIVITIES: 1. Research the geologic history of camels and rhinoceroses in North America. 2. Find out how the development of prairies influenced changes in animals.

ANSWER KEY:
Page 10 1. Glyptodont 2. Eohippus **Study Question:** marsupials, primates, insectivores, rodents, and some carnivores
Page 10a 1. A. Planetetherium B. boa constrictor C. Diatryma D. Eohippus E. Glyptodont F. Brontotherium 2. a. large beak and sharp claws b. armored body and club-like tail c. constricting power 3. Brontotherium 4. The first horses were smaller and had feet with several digits 5. boa constrictor

Page 11 - CENOZOIC ERA *Quaternary Period*

CONCEPT: According to the geologic scale, we are presently living in the Recent epoch of the Quaternary period of the Cenozoic Era; the Quaternary period includes the Great Ice Age.

BACKGROUND INFORMATION: The Quaternary period includes a span of years from about two million years ago to the present. It is often divided into two epochs — Pleistocene and Recent. The Pleistocene is also known as the Great Ice Age. During the Ice Age, massive sheets of ice covered large areas of the world. Many plants and animals of previous periods became extinct. There were four major periods of ice and cold and three intervening warmer periods during which the ice melted. Throughout the Quaternary period, there existed a great variety of animals all over the world. Some examples include elephants, horses, buffaloes, camels, wild pigs, carnivores, ground sloths, reindeer, and Arctic foxes. During the Pleistocene epoch, many animals underwent evolutionary development because of changes in climate. Elephants, such as the woolly mammoth, were well suited to life where winters were cold. The woolly mammoth looked like a modern day elephant with long, shaggy hair. It had such big teeth that there were never more than eight teeth in its mouth at one time. Its tusks of ivory were sought by Chinese traders during the fourth century. There are still numerous skeletons and tusks of these animals in the frozen soil of Alaska and Siberia. Great herds of royal bison roamed the plain areas. Some of these bison had a hornspread of 1.8m. A fierce-looking carnivore, the Smilodon or stabbing cat, often called a saber-toothed tiger, had two large teeth or fangs in its upper jaw. It was about the size of a lion and had very powerful jaws. Remains of the stabbing cat and other extinct carnivores are frequently found in great numbers in the La Brea Tar Pits in California. Stone artifacts and fossils have been found providing evidence that early man flourished during the Quaternary Period of the Cenozoic Era.

ENRICHMENT ACTIVITIES: 1. Find out about the great ground sloths and the dire wolf, *Canis dirus*. 2. Find out about the development of today's rhinoceros.

ANSWER KEY:
Page 11 1. woolly mammoth — tusks, Smilodon — teeth and claws, royal bison — horns, early man — weapons 2. Woolly mammoths and royal bison had thick coats of hair for protection against the cold. **Study Question:** Eohippus was very small, about the size of a small dog, and had four toes on each front foot and three toes on each back foot; Mesohippus was the size of a large dog, and had three toes on each foot with the middle toe much larger than the other two; Meryohippus was larger in size, and had three toes but only the middle toes now touched the ground when it walked or ran; Pliopippus was quite tall, and had teeth specialized for biting and grinding grass. It had one very large toe on each foot and this toe helped it to run more rapidly than its ancestors. The nail of the very large toe became the hoof of the modern horse, Equus.
Page 11a 1. Quaternary 2. C. early man D. Smilodon or stabbing cat 3. B. woolly mammoth C. early man E. royal bison 4. a. 1 b. 2 c. 3 d. 1 e. 4 f. 2 g. 4 5. a. food b. clothing c. weapons

Page 12 PREHISTORIC PEOPLE

CONCEPTS: 1. Prehistoric human remains are among some of the rarest of fossils. 2. By linking stone artifacts and human fossils, scientists have been able to partially reconstruct the appearance and daily life of prehistoric people.

BACKGROUND INFORMATION: Bones of our ancestors are among the rarest of fossils. Prehistoric people were never very numerous and therefore did not leave massive numbers of fossils as did the invertebrate animals. A complete fossil record of the development of man is not available and many portions of the family tree are missing. Also, some scientists interpret the fossil record differently and there is some disagreement on the age and relationships of the earliest fossils. One such fossil is that of *Australopithecus afarensis*. While generally thought to be an early human-type organism, there is no agreement on this fossil's position in the human family tree. *A. africanus* lived from about 3 million to 2 million years ago and, while still retaining many ape-like features, these prehistoric people walked upright and possessed a flatter face than that of an ape. About 2.2 million years ago, an early human, *A. robustus*, appeared. These individuals were markedly different from any contemporaries. The skull was massive and the molar teeth huge. The species vanished and does not form a link to the first human, *Homo habilis*. These early humans were not unlike *A. africanus* but had a larger brain size. Stone implements found with the fossils indicate that they were able to shape stones to use for cutting and chopping. *Homo erectus* was on the earth from about 1.6 to

0.4 million years ago. Fossils of this species have been found in China as well as Africa. The brain size is similar to modern humans. *H. erectus* was able to control fire. The skulls of early *Homo sapiens* have a more prominent bulge in the forehead to accommodate a larger brain. The brow ridges are less massive. In general, this species is more modern in appearance than early *H. erectus*. The Neanderthal people, *Homo sapiens neanderthalensis*, lived in Europe 130,000 to 35,000 years ago. They were known to inhabit caves, and grave sites indicate that they buried their dead with ritual objects such as flowers, tools, and food. The skull was less modern in appearance due to its elongation from front to back and the large brow ridges. About 30,000 years ago modern humans, *Homo sapiens sapiens*, appeared in Europe. Best known of these are the Cro-Magnon fossils of France.

ENRICHMENT ACTIVITIES: 1. Research how these fossils are associated with prehistoric humans, *Ramapithecus* and *Sivapithecus*. 2. Find out about the work of the Leakeys in Africa.

ANSWER KEY:
Page 12 1. *A. afarenis*; 2. Neanderthals had elongated skulls and large brow ridges **Study Question:** The Peking people were a form of *H. erectus*; Cro-Magnon people were of the *Homo sapiens* species.
Page 12a 1. Answers will vary - see Transparency, page 12. 2. a. *H. erectus* b. *H. sapiens* (Neanderthal) c. *H. habilis* 3. early *Homo sapiens* 4. *H. habilis* and *H. erectus* 5. a. 2-3 million years ago b. .4 to 1.6 million years ago c. 22 to 1.6 million years ago 6. prominent brow ridges

A LAST LOOK - PART I
A. 1. Photographs do not belong. Casts and imprints are fossils. Photographs are not.
2. Boa constrictor does not belong. The royal bison and woolly mammoth lived during the Quaternary period of the Cenozoic Era. The boa constrictor was a Tertiary animal.
3. Ankylosaurus does not belong. Pteranodon and Icthyornis are reptile-like birds. Ankylosaurus is an armored dinosaur.
4. Cambrian period does not belong. Mississippian and Pennsylvanian are Carboniferous periods. Cambrian is not.
5. Scorpion does not belong. Trilobite and brachiopod are early marine invertebrates. The scorpion is a land invertebrate.
6. Tulip tree does not belong. Tree ferns and scale trees were abundant in Carboniferous swamps. Tulip trees were not.
7. Tyrannosaurus does not belong. It is a carnivore. Brontosaurus and Stegosaurus are herbivores.
8. Hesperonis does not belong. It is a reptile-like bird. The other two are prehistoric people.
9. Crinoid does not belong. It is an early marine animal. Conifers and cycads are plants.
10. Eohippus does not belong. It is a mammal, the forerunner of the horse. Tyrannosaurus and Ankylosaurus are dinosaurs.

NOTE: These are suggested answers, each determined by a specific viewpoint. Since more than one correct answer is possible, accept any reasonable answer student can justify.

B. 1. fossils 5. Fish 8. ice
2. horse 6. coal 9. man
3. fins 7. flying 10. dinosaur
4. trees

A LAST LOOK - PART II
1. A. dragonfly 4. A. woolly mammoth 7. A. trilobite 10. A. Diatryma
B. Pennsylvanian B. Quaternary B. Cambrian B. Tertiary
2. A. shark 5. A. Dimetrodon 8. A. broadleaf fern 11. A. Stegosaurus
B. Mississippian B. Permian B. Triassic B. Jurassic
3. A. cycad 6. A. deciduous trees 9. A. early man 12. A. lungfish
B. Jurassic B. Cretaceous B. Quaternary B. Pennsylvanian

A LAST LOOK - PART III
A. 1. j 5. h 8. c
2. g 6. i 9. e
3. f 7. d 10. a
4. b

B. 1. Devonian 5. Devonian 8. water
2. coal 6. carnivorous 9. reptiles
3. latest 7. Mammals 10. epochs
4. conifers

A LAST LOOK - PART IV
A. The cartoon illustrates the theory that the dinosaurs died out because: 1. when the climate and the lush, green plants disappeared, there was not enough food for the herbivores; 2. when the herbivores died out, there was nothing for the carnivores to eat, and so they, too, disappeared.

B. 1. The center drawing is incorrect, since it is an example of the preservation of actual remains, not a mold or cast.
2. Only the sketch on the right is a primitive plant. The others are forms of marine animal life.
3. Early man did not live during the Mesozoic Era.
4. The Placodus is a reptile, not a mammal. Eohippus and Planetetherium are mammals.

C.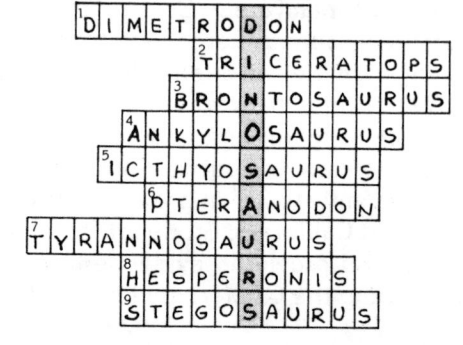

The following section contains the student worksheets. Each worksheet should be introduced by the corresponding transparency found at the back of this book.

Formation of Fossils

A. _____

insect in 1. _____   shark tooth    mammoth bone from 2. _____

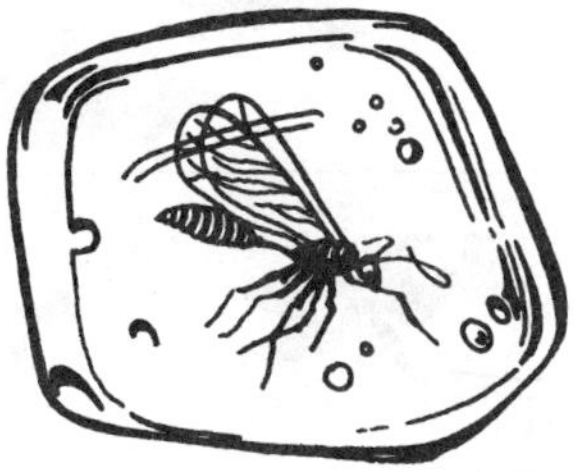

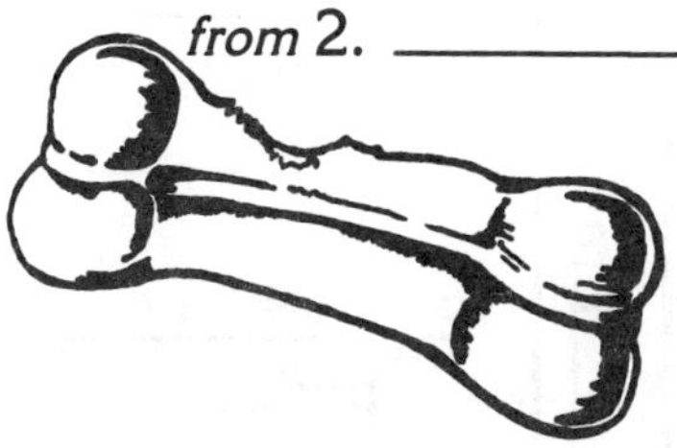

B. _____

3. _____   4.  _____   5. _____

C. _____

6. _____   7. _____

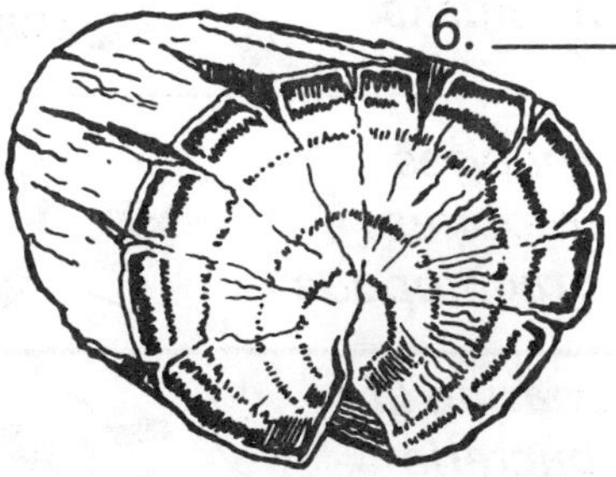

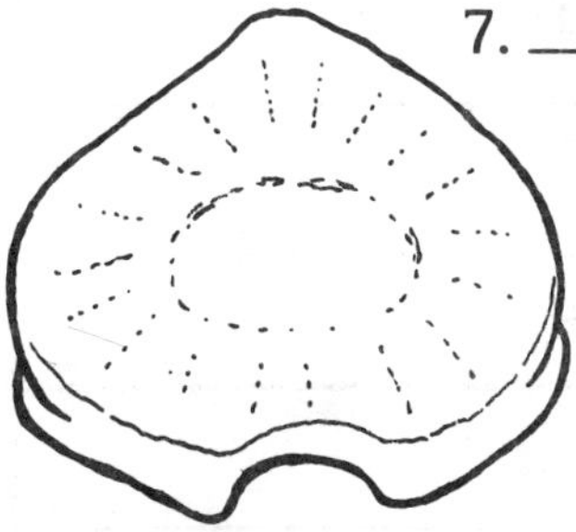

1. On lines A, B, and C, write the ways fossils are formed.
2. Complete the missing labels above numbered 1—7.
3. Find the description in Column B that describes each phrase in Column A. Write the number of that description in the space provided.

Column A	Column B
_____ a. an animal footprint	1. Preservation of actual remains
_____ b. a skeleton	2. Molds, casts, and imprints
_____ c. animal frozen in ice	3. Replacement by mineral matter
_____ d. a "stone-like" tree trunk	
_____ e. an outline of fish scales	

Copyright © 1986 — Milliken Publishing Co. All rights reserved.   Fossils and Prehistoric Life 1a.

Geological Time Scale — I

	TIME UNITS	YEARS AGO	REPRESENTATIVE LIFE	
Era	1. _____ period	230,000,000 to 280,000,000	many land plants and animals	
	2. _____ period	280,000,000 to 310,000,000	reptiles insects spiders	
	3. _____ period	310,000,000 to 345,000,000	many crinoids sharks swamp forests	
	4. _____ period	345,000,000 to 400,000,000	amphibians land plants	
	5. _____ period	400,000,000 to 430,000,000	coral scorpions lungfish	
9.	6. _____ period	430,000,000 to 500,000,000	crinoids fish mollusks	
	7. _____ period	500,000,000 to 570,000,000	sponges trilobites brachiopods	
	8. _____ Era	570,000,000 to 4,500,000,000	marine life bacteria algae	

1. In the chart above, write in the era and period names.

2. What is the approximate age of the appearance of these organisms?

   a. oldest trilobite _____

   b. simplest bacteria and algae _____

   c. oldest scorpions _____

   d. oldest reptiles _____

   e. oldest vertebrate _____

3. During which period did each of these events take place?

   a. first amphibian appears _____

   b. appearance of first reptiles _____

   c. land invertebrates appear _____

   d. first fish make appearance _____

   e. formation of coal swamps _____

2a. Fossils and Prehistoric Life

Geological Time Scale — II

	TIME UNITS	YEARS AGO	REPRESENTATIVE LIFE
Era 7.	1. _____ period	Present to 2,000,000	ice ages modern mammals
	2. _____ period	2,000,000 to 65,000,000	prehistoric humans appear (Pliocene) many mammals
Era 6.	3. _____ period	65,000,000 to 135,000,000	flowering plants many dinosaurs
	4. _____ period	135,000,000 to 180,000,000	birds many dinosaurs
	5. _____ period	180,000,000 to 230,000,000	mammals dinosaurs conifers

1. Write in the era and period names in the chart above.
2. During which period did each of these events take place?

    a. appearance of first mammals _____

    b. prehistoric people appear _____

    c. dinosaurs die out _____

    d. first birds appear _____

    e. flowering plants rise _____

    f. appearance of modern domestic animals _____

3. What is the approximate age of each of these events?

    a. dinosaurs die out _____

    b. flowering plants begin _____

    c. conifer trees rise _____

    d. birds appear _____

Copyright © 1986 — Milliken Publishing Co. All rights reserved.

Fossils and Prehistoric Life 3a.

Geological Events — Timeline

ERA	PERIOD	YEARS AGO	GEOLOGICAL EVENT
CENOZOIC	Quaternary	Present to 2,000,000	Continental glaciation
CENOZOIC	Tertiary	2,000,000 to 65,000,000	Volcanoes in western United States
MESOZOIC	Cretaceous	65,000,000 to 135,000,000	Beginning of Rocky Mountains
MESOZOIC	Jurassic	135,000,000 to 180,000,000	Rise of the Sierra Nevada Mts.
MESOZOIC	Triassic	180,000,000 to 230,000,000	North America, South America, and Africa begin splitting apart.
PALEOZOIC	Permian	230,000,000 to 280,000,000	Ice age in southern hemisphere; shallow seas in North America evaporate.
PALEOZOIC	Pennsylvanian	280,000,000 to 310,000,000	Extensive coal-forming swamps in eastern United States
PALEOZOIC	Mississippian	310,000,000 to 345,000,000	Large areas of North American continent submerged under water
PALEOZOIC	Devonian	345,000,000 to 400,000,000	White Mountains formed
PALEOZOIC	Silurian	400,000,000 to 430,000,000	Northern United States becomes dry; shallow seas evaporate.
PALEOZOIC	Ordovician	430,000,000 to 500,000,000	Beginning of Appalachian Mountains
PALEOZOIC	Cambrian	500,000,000 to 570,000,000	Deposition of sediments in inland seas
PRE-CAMBRIAN		570,000,000 to 4,500,000,000	Extensive volcanic activity

1. Name the oldest mountains in North America. _____
2. During which period did most of our coal fields have their beginnings? _____
3. Which era was the longest in duration? _____
4. During the recent _____ period, large areas of Washington and Oregon were covered with volcanic materials.
5. Large areas of central United States were underwater during the _____ and the _____ periods.

3b. Fossils and Prehistoric Life

Paleozoic Era — I

A. _____ B. _____ C. _____ D. _____

E. _____
F. _____
G. _____
H. _____
I. _____
J. _____
K. _____
L. _____

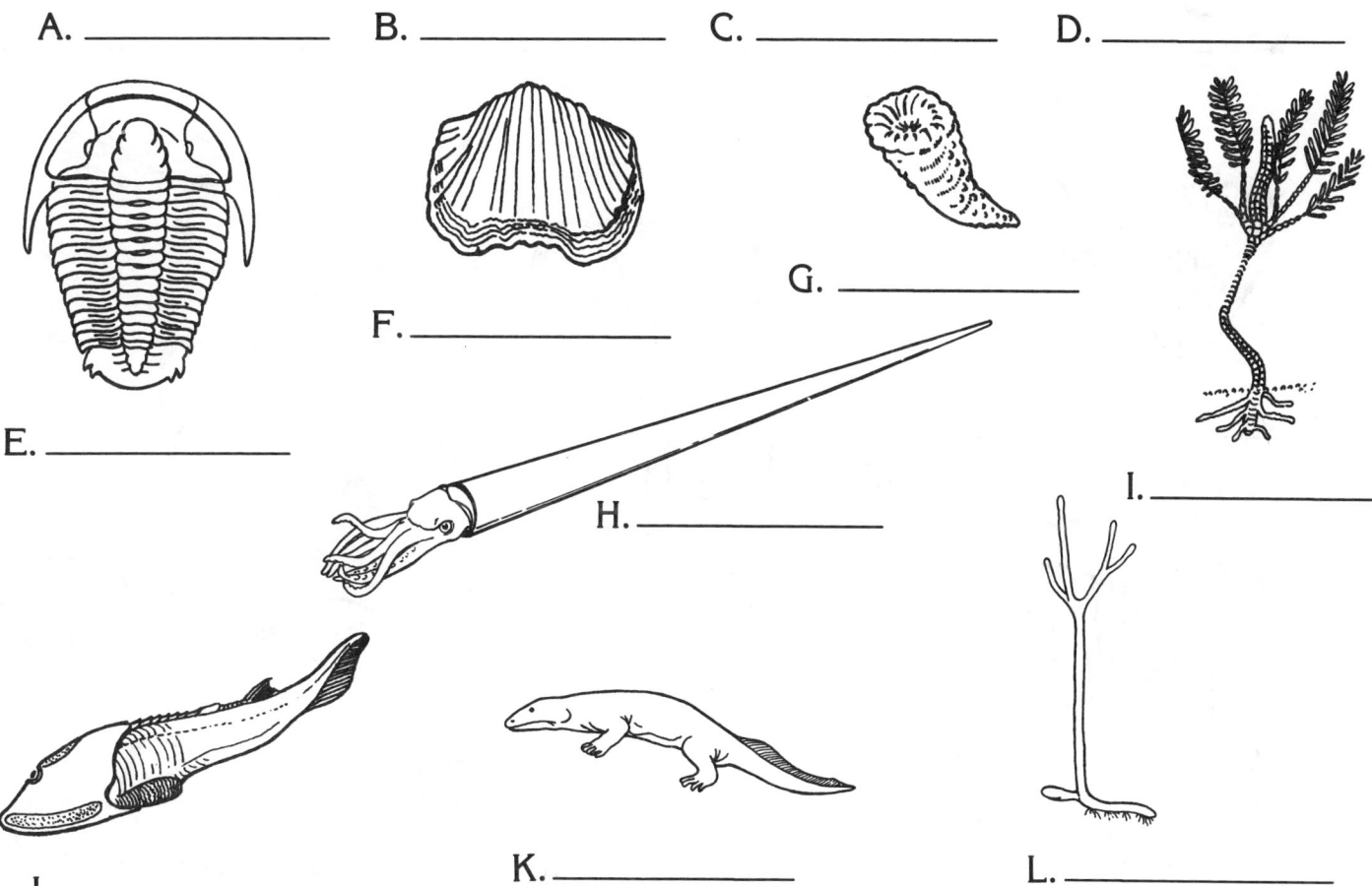

1. Name the first four periods of the Paleozoic Era on lines A, B, C, and D.
2. Label the invertebrate marine life.
3. Label the vertebrate life and plant life.
4. Match Column B with Column A. After each match, write C, O, S, or D to identify the geological period during which each appeared.

Column A	Column B
_____ a. clam-like shell _____	1. coral
_____ b. marine arthropod _____	2. cephalopod
_____ c. shark _____	3. trilobite
_____ d. coral reef _____	4. brachiopod
_____ e. salamander _____	5. primitive amphibian
_____ f. squid _____	6. crinoid
_____ g. "sea-lily" animal _____	7. primitive land plant
_____ h. tree-like plant _____	8. primitive vertebrate

Copyright © 1986 — Milliken Publishing Co. All rights reserved.   Fossils and Prehistoric Life 4a.

Paleozoic Era — II

A. _____   B. _____   C. _____

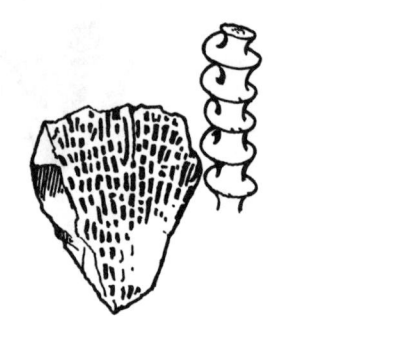

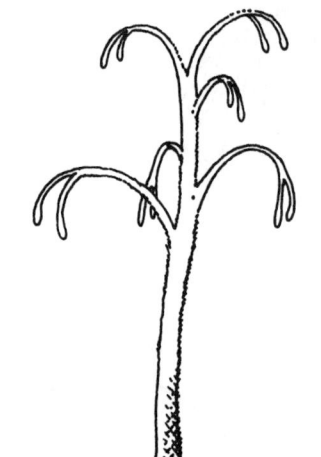

D. _____

F. _____

E. _____

G. _____

H. _____

1. Label the three latest periods of the Paleozoic Era on lines A, B, and C.
2. Label the plant life shown above.
3. Label the vertebrates and the invertebrates shown above.
4. Match Column B with Column A. After each match, write M., Pa., or Per. to identify the geological period.

Column A	Column B
_____ a. scale tree _____ _____ e. centipedes _____ _____ b. shell crusher _____ _____ f. corkscrew _____ _____ c. fin-back reptile _____ _____ g. dragonfly _____ _____ d. lace-type _____	1. bryozoa 2. Dimetrodon 3. primitive arthropod 4. Lepidodendron 5. shark

5a. Fossils and Prehistoric Life

Carboniferous Swamp

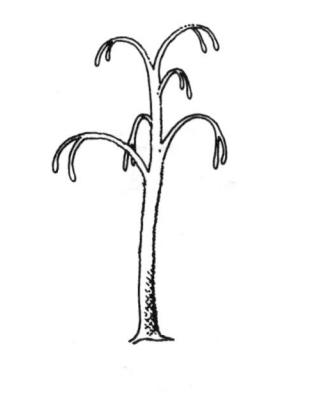

A. _____

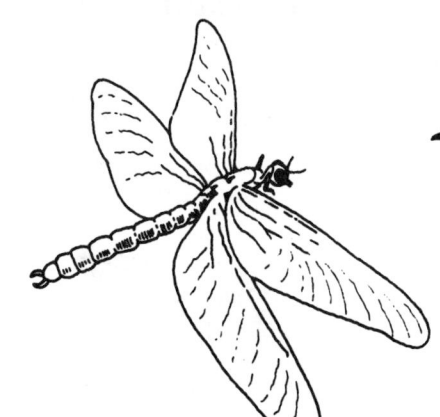

B. _____

C. _____

D. _____

E. _____

F. _____

1. Label the plants and animals indicated in the drawing.
2. How did the plant life of this period differ from that of modern plants? _____
   _____
   _____
3. What is a general characteristic of the insects in this period? _____
   _____
4. What were the probable climatic conditions of the Carboniferous period? _____
   _____
   _____
5. What were the probable causes for the disappearance of the Carboniferous swamps? _____
   _____
   _____

Mesozoic Era
Triassic period

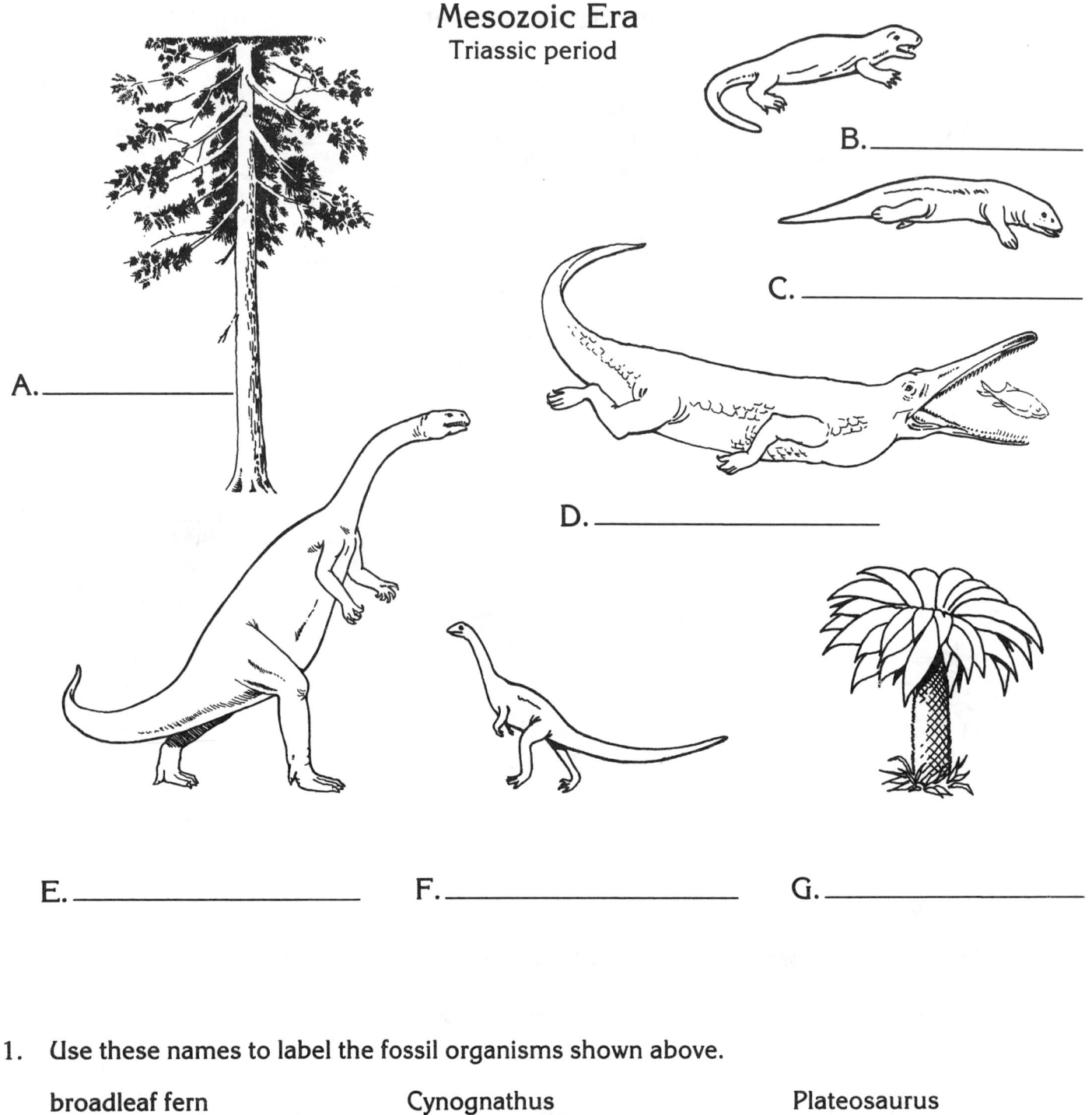

A. _____
B. _____
C. _____
D. _____
E. _____
F. _____
G. _____

1. Use these names to label the fossil organisms shown above.

   broadleaf fern   Cynognathus   Plateosaurus
   Podokesaurus   conifer   Phytosaurus
   Placodus

2. Which Triassic reptile resembled a modern crocodile? _____

3. The _____ was a small mammal-like, carnivorous reptile.

4. The short neck, thick body, and paddle-like flippers of _____ resemble those of a walrus.

5. Which of these Triassic reptiles was the smallest? _____

   the tallest? _____

7a. Fossils and Prehistoric Life   Copyright © 1986 — Milliken Publishing Co. All rights reserved.

Mesozoic Era
Family Tree of the Dinosaurs

Cretaceous period	Tyrannosaurus, Ankylosaurus
Jurassic period	Ornithischia *Bird-hipped*, Saurischia *Reptile-hipped*, **Birds** Archaeopteryx
Triassic period	**Dinosaurs**, **Mammals** Therapsida *Cynognathus*, Thecodontia *Saltoposuchus*
Permian period	Cotylosaurs *Stem reptiles*

1. What is the probable reptile ancestor of the mammals? _____
2. During which period did the first mammal appear? _____
3. Tyrannosaurus belongs to which group of dinosaurs? _____
4. During which period did the birds arise? _____
5. An example of an ornithischia dinosaur is the _____
6. The _____ was the ancestor to the dinosaurs and probably the birds.

Copyright © 1986 — Milliken Publishing Co. All rights reserved.

Fossils and Prehistoric Life 7b.

Mesozoic Era

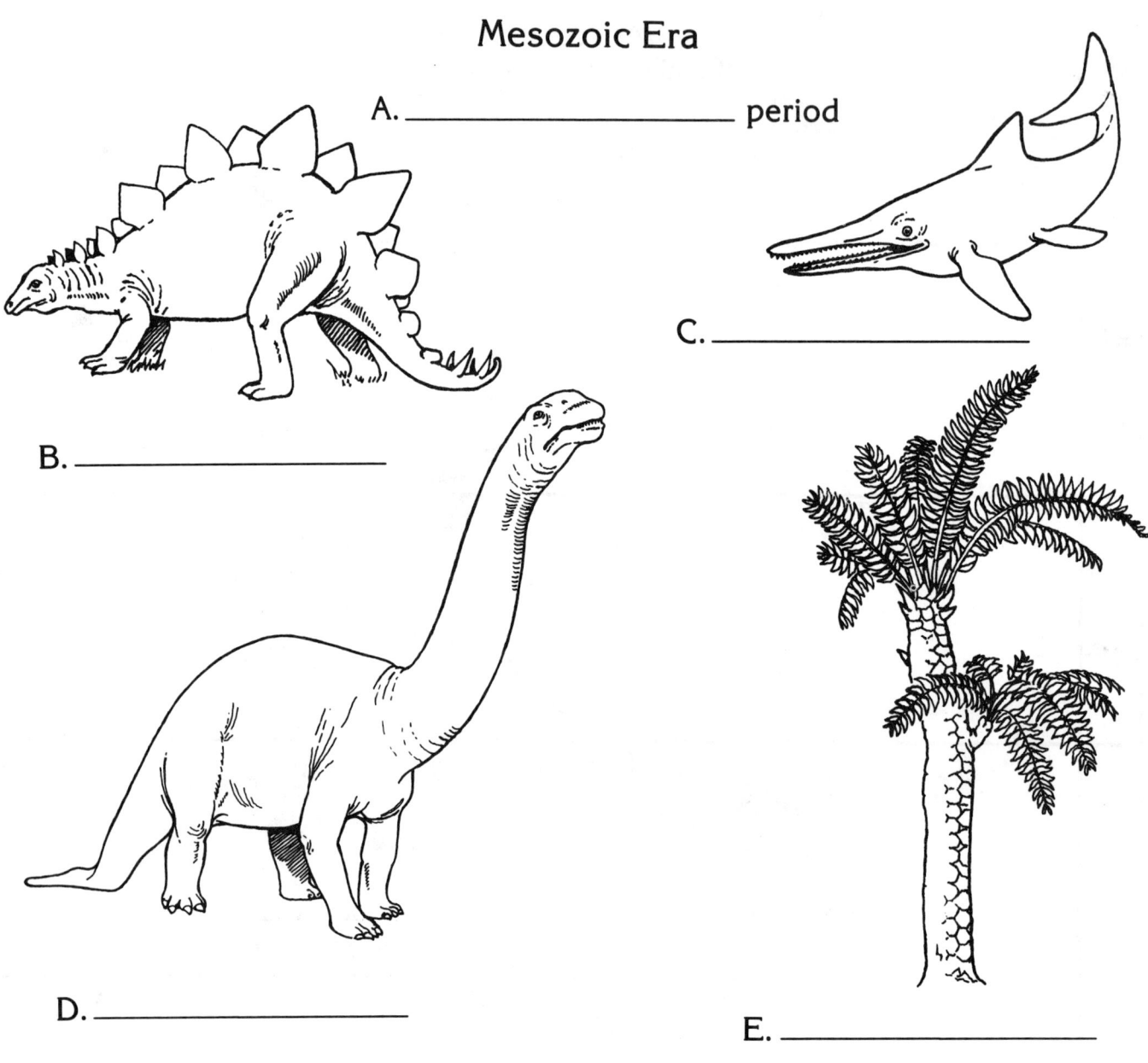

A. _____ period
B. _____
C. _____
D. _____
E. _____

1. Name the middle period of the Mesozoic Era on line A.
2. Identify and label the animals and plants shown above.
3. All the animals shown above are classified as _____ .

        mammals   reptiles   invertebrates

4. Match Column B with Column A. Write your answer in the space provided.

Column A		Column B
_____ 1. a marine reptile	_____ 5. weighed over 30 tons	a. Ichthyosaurus
_____ 2. palm-like seed plant	_____ 6. grew over 30m tall	b. Stegosaurus
_____ 3. an amphibious reptile	_____ 7. dolphin-like reptile	c. cycad
_____ 4. an armored, plated reptile	_____ 8. used tail for defense	d. Brontosaurus

8a. Fossils and Prehistoric Life

Mesozoic Era
Jurassic period
Age of large reptiles and insects

Some characteristics of reptiles:
    a. cold-blooded vertebrates with lungs
    b. bony skeleton
    c. body covered with scales or horny plates
    d. a three-chambered heart (2 atria and 1 ventricle)

1. Which are reptiles? (Circle your answers.)
    a. snakes   e. sharks   i. crocodiles
    b. earthworms   f. alligators   j. salamanders
    c. lizards   g. frogs   k. dinosaurs
    d. turtles   h. wrens

Some characteristics of insects:
    a. three separate body regions — head, thorax, abdomen
    b. a pair of feelers attached to head
    c. one or two pairs of wings attached to body
    d. breathe through branching tubes connected to openings located on each side of abdomen and thorax
    e. three pairs of legs attached to thorax

2. Which are insects? (Circle your answers.)
    a. grasshoppers   e. moths   i. millipedes
    b. spiders   f. centipedes   j. butterflies
    c. eels   g. flies   k. caddis-flies
    d. termites   h. beetles

Prehistoric Animal Names from the Greek Language

Greek Word	English Meaning	Greek Word	English Meaning	Greek Word	English Meaning
a. sauros	reptile	e. bronto	thunder	i. daktylos	finger
b. ichthus	fish	f. podos	foot	j. archaeos	old, ancient
c. deinos	terrible	g. odon	tooth	k. pteryx	wing
d. plesios	almost	h. pteron	wing (feather)	l. stegos	roof

3. What is the literal translation of the following prehistoric animals?

    a. Brontosaurus means — _____

    b. Ichthyosaurus means — _____

    c. dinosaur means — _____

    d. pterodactyl means — _____

    e. Plesiosaurus means — _____

4. Write the name of each prehistoric animal next to the meaning of its name.

    a. fish reptile — _____   c. wing toothed — _____

    b. old wing — _____   d. roof reptile — _____

    Archaeopteryx   Stegosaurus   Ichthyosaurus   Trachodon   Triceratops   Pteranodon

Mesozoic Era

A. _____ period

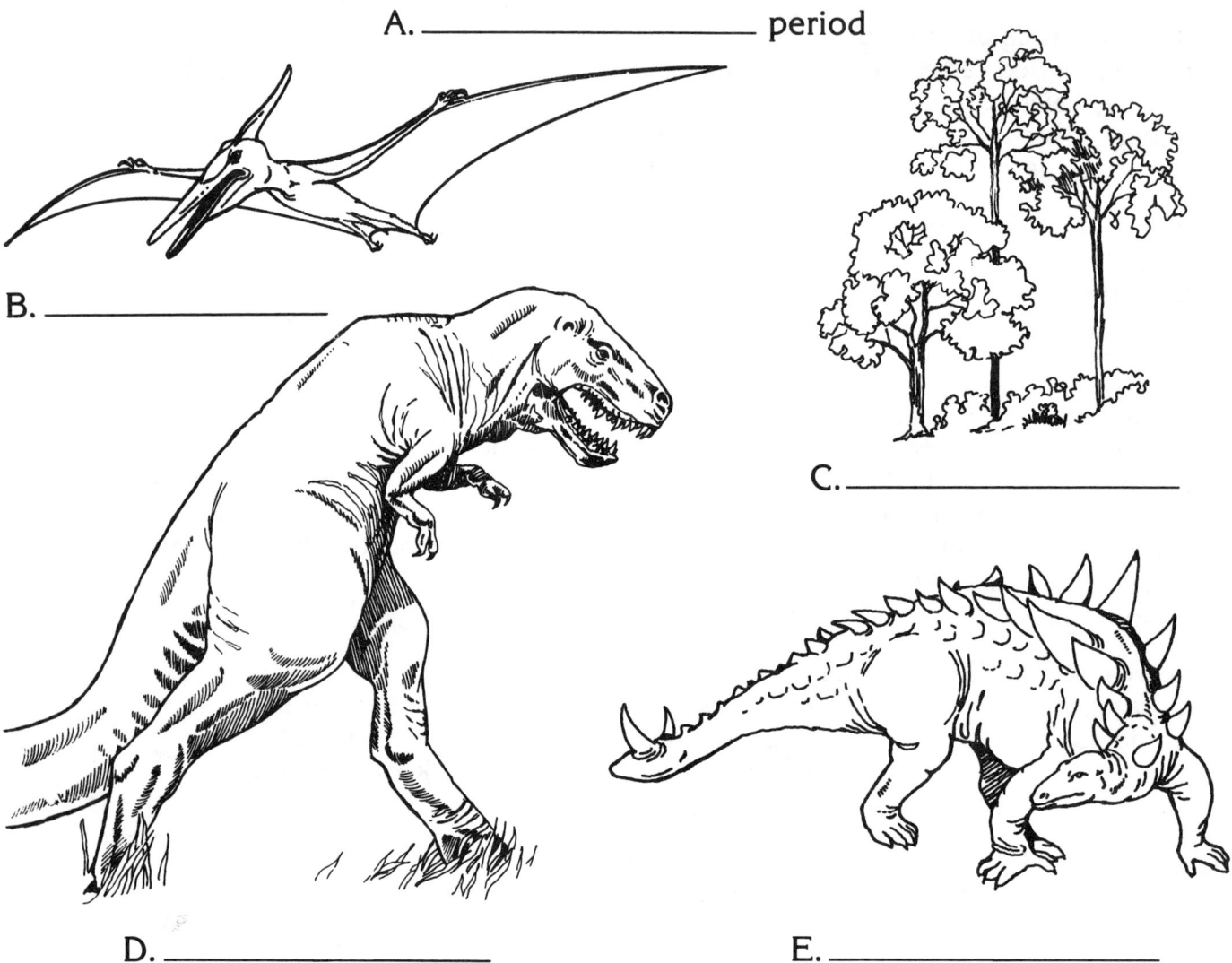

B. _____

C. _____

D. _____   E. _____

1. Name the last period of the Mesozoic Era on line A.
2. Identify and label the animals and plant life shown above.
3. From the picture above, the reptile that probably attacked other reptiles was the _____ .
       Pteranodon   Tyrannosaurus   Ankylosaurus
4. Match Column B with Column A. Write your answer in the space provided.

Column A		Column B
____ 1. an armored reptile	____ 5. fish-seeking, soaring reptile	a. Tyrannosaurus
____ 2. 16m long and 6m tall	____ 6. a defense of spiked body and tail	b. Pteranodon
____ 3. magnolias, tulip trees, and ivy	____ 7. dinosaur with large head and big teeth	c. flowering plants/trees
____ 4. a powerful, carnivorous reptile	____ 8. an herbivorous reptile	d. Ankylosaurus

9a. Fossils and Prehistoric Life

Mesozoic Era
Cretaceous period
First appearance of "true" birds

Some characteristics of Prehistoric "reptile-like" birds:
1. Jaws were without bills but filled with teeth.
2. Scales covered the head with partial feathers on body and wings.
3. Both wings had "fingers" with claws.
4. Tails were long and slender with feathers protruding from both sides.
5. Body sizes varied.

Some Prehistoric "reptile-like" birds:

Ichthyornis
1. size of a pigeon
2. skillful flier
3. small, weak legs
4. looked like modern tern

Hesperonis
1. size of a small seal
2. undeveloped wings, could not fly
3. legs set well to back of body
4. a strong swimmer
5. beak lined with sharp teeth
6. looked like a modern loon

Pteranodons
1. size of a turkey
2. wingspread of nearly 7.5m
3. head had a distinctive crest
4. able to soar in air for long periods
5. had claws on wings, tiny hind limbs
6. toothless bill, ate fish

Diatryma
1. stood nearly 2.5m tall
2. head as large as that of a horse
3. sharp bill
4. powerful legs, very fast runner
5. flightless

1. Fill in the missing words. Prehistoric birds looked more like _____ than modern birds. They had fingers with _____ on their _____ and jaws filled with _____.

2. Identify each bird by its description. Write I, P, H, D in the space before each description.
   _____ 1. had a very large set of wings
   _____ 2. moved well in water
   _____ 3. had a very large head
   _____ 4. small size and legs
   _____ 5. had ostrich-like characteristics

   I = Ichthyornis
   P = Pteranodons
   H = Hesperonis
   D = Diatryma

Some characteristics of Modern Day birds:
1. Body is covered with feathers.
2. Forelimbs develop into wings.
3. Bones are hollow.
4. Body temperature is constant.
5. Birds lay shelled eggs.

Some Modern Day birds:

Long-legged Waders
herons   ibises
storks   flamingos

Birds of Prey
falcons   hawks
vultures

Fowl-like Birds
turkeys   partridges
quails   pheasants

3. Fill in the missing words. Modern day birds are light in weight due partially to their _____ being hollow and their bodies covered with _____. Like most reptiles, baby birds are brought forth from _____.

4. Identify each of these modern day birds: Write S, V, O, F, T or Fl in each space.
   _____ 1. a large scavenger bird
   _____ 2. usually pink in color
   _____ 3. a favorite bird in November

   S = stork   F = falcon
   V = vulture   T = turkey
   O = owl   Fl = flamingo

Cenozoic Era
Tertiary period

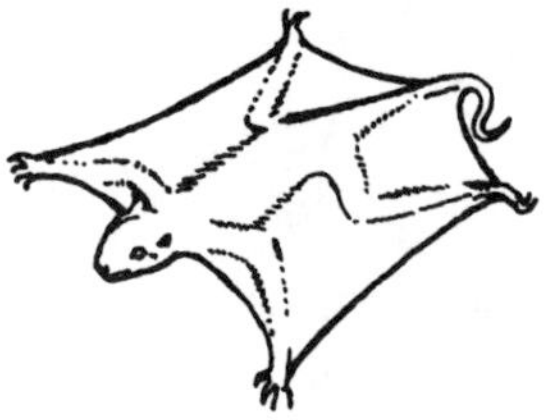

A. _____
Paleocene epoch

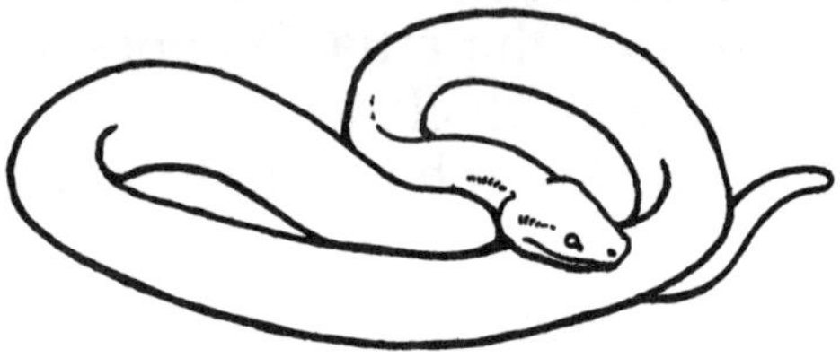

B. _____
Paleocene epoch

C. _____
Eocene epoch

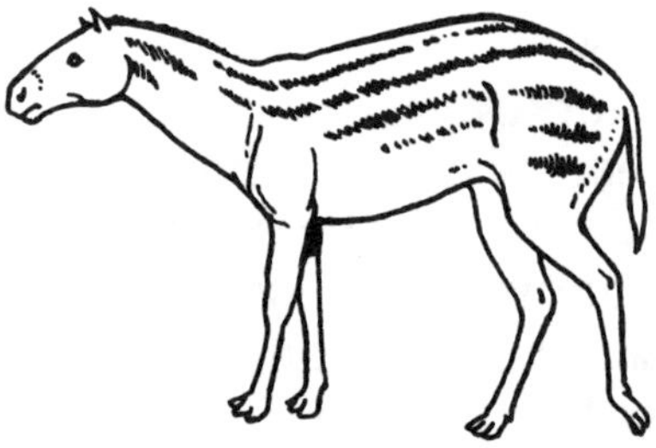

D. _____
Miocene epoch

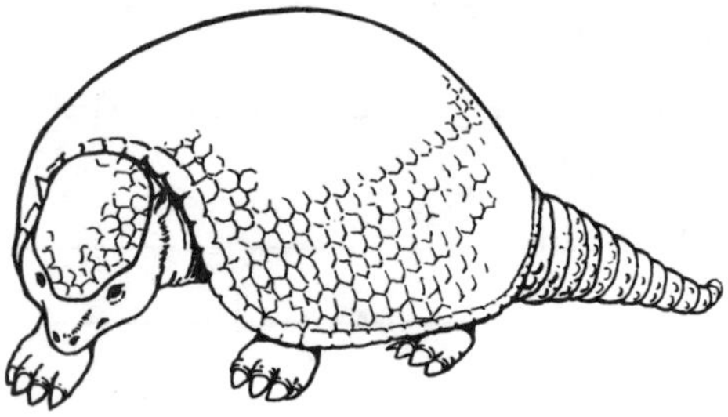

E. _____
Pliocene epoch

F. _____
Oligocene epoch

1. Use these names to label the animals shown above.
   - Eohippus
   - Diatryma
   - Brontotherium
   - Planetetherium
   - boa constrictor
   - Glyptodont

2. What was the defense of each of these animals against predators?

   a. Diatryma _____

   b. Glyptodont _____

   c. boa constrictor _____

3. The _____ was a large mammal resembling an elephant and a rhinoceros.

4. How did the first horses differ from the horses of today? _____
   _____

5. Which Tertiary reptile is similar to its modern form? _____

10a. Fossils and Prehistoric Life   Copyright © 1986 — Milliken Publishing Co. All rights reserved.

Cenozoic Era

A. _____ period

B. _____

C. _____

D. _____

E. _____

1. Name the last period of the Cenozoic Era on Line A.
2. Label the carnivorous mammals shown above.
3. Label the herbivorous mammals shown above.
4. Match Column B with Column A.

Column A (Today)		Column B (Ancestor)
_____ a. oxen	_____ e. Homo sapiens	1. royal bison
_____ b. pachyderm	_____ f. mastodon	2. woolly mammoth
_____ c. puma	_____ g. able to reason	3. stabbing cat
_____ d. long-horned cattle		4. early man

5. Name three things early man might have used from the animals of his time.

   a. _____   b. _____   c. _____

Prehistoric People

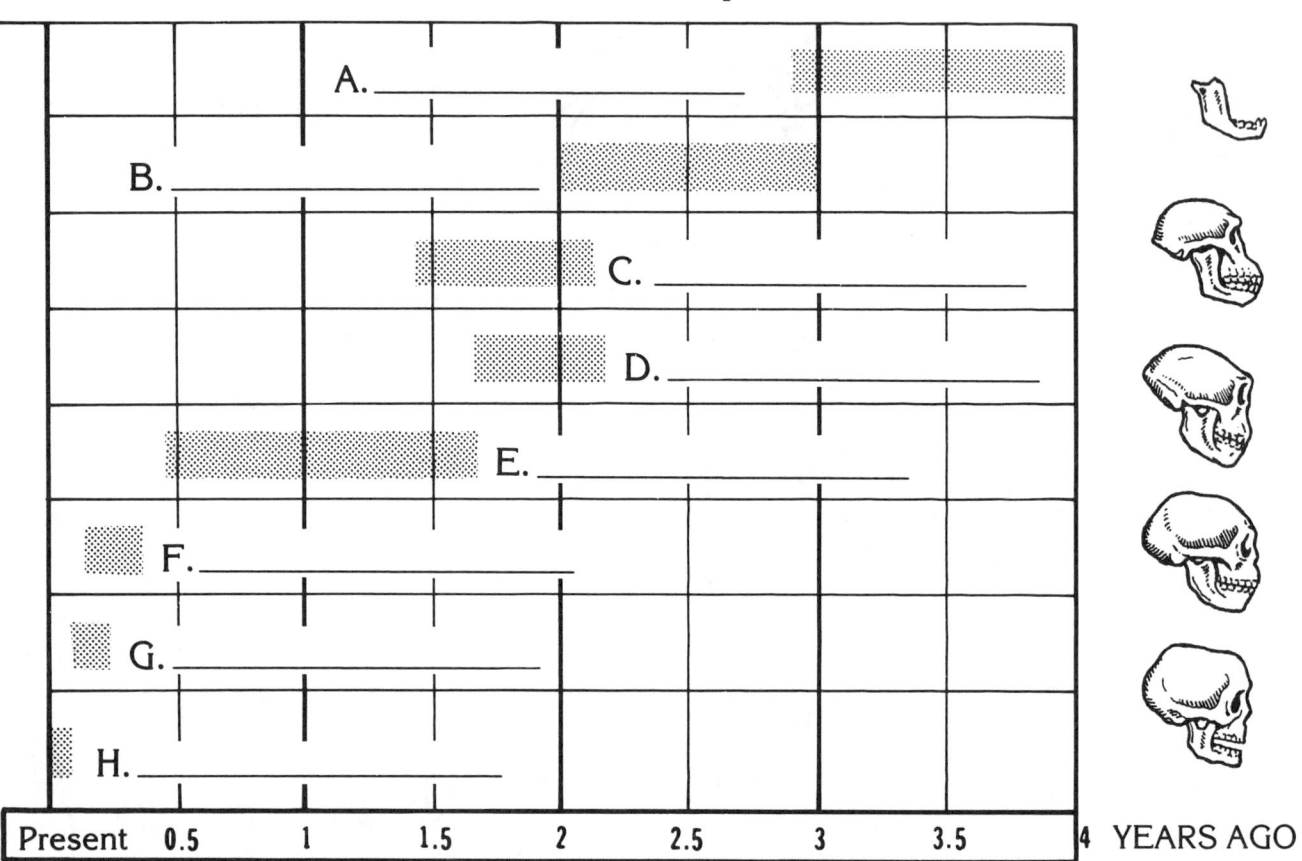

A. _____
B. _____
C. _____
D. _____
E. _____
F. _____
G. _____
H. _____

Present 0.5 1 1.5 2 2.5 3 3.5 4 YEARS AGO

1. Write one characteristic for each prehistoric human shown above.

2. Which prehistoric people were the first to:

   a. control fire _____

   b. hold ritual burial ceremonies _____

   c. use simple stone tools _____

3. Which prehistoric people were probably most similar to humans in appearance?

   _____

4. Which of the prehistoric people of the genus **Homo** inhabited the earth at the same time as **Australopithecus robustus**? _____

5. When did these prehistoric people live?

   a. **Australopithecus africanus** _____

   b. **Homo erectus** _____

   c. **Homo habilis** _____

6. What facial feature did many of the prehistoric people have that is similar to modern apes? _____

12a. Fossils and Prehistoric Life   Copyright © 1986 — Milliken Publishing Co. All rights reserved.

A Last Look — Part I

A. In each of the following groups one item does not belong. Circle that item and in the space provided explain why it does not belong.

1. casts — photographs — imprints

2. woolly mammoth — royal bison — boa constrictor

3. Ankylosaurus — Icthyornis — Pteranodon

4. Mississippian period — Pennsylvanian period — Cambrian period

5. brachiopod — scorpion — trilobite

6. tree fern — tulip tree — scale tree

7. Tyrannosaurus — Stegosaurus — Brontosaurus

8. Homo erectus — Hesperonis — Australopithecus africanus

9. conifer — cycad — crinoid

10. Eohippus — Tyrannosaurus — Ankylosaurus

B. Write the word that will make each sentence a true statement.

1. _____ are evidence of ancient life.
2. Eohippus was the first ancestor of the _____.
3. Reptiles of the Permian period had large _____ on their backs.
4. Petrified wood is the fossil remains of ancient _____.
5. _____ were the first vertebrates to appear.
6. Ancient swamp vegetation helped form the huge _____ deposits of today.
7. The Pteranodon was a large _____ reptile.
8. During the Pleistocene epoch of the Quaternary period, massive sheets of _____ covered large areas of the world.
9. Neanderthal man was the first to be classified by scientists as a _____ rather than man-ape.
10. Stegosaurus was a _____ with a double row of bony plates on its back.

A Last Look — Part II

On line **A**, name the fossil plant or animal shown.
In part **B**, circle the geological time period in which it appeared.

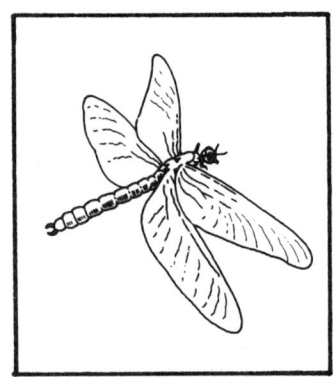  

1. A. _____
   B. Silurian
      Pennsylvanian

2. A. _____
   B. Mississippian
      Cambrian

3. A. _____
   B. Jurassic
      Ordovician

4. A. _____
   B. Cretaceous
      Quaternary

  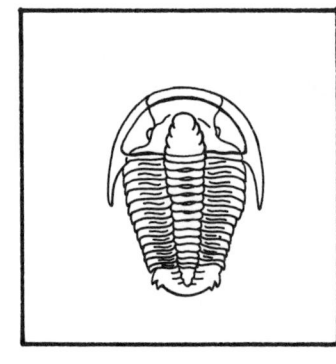 

5. A. _____
   B. Permian
      Tertiary

6. A. _____
   B. Permian
      Cretaceous

7. A. _____
   B. Cambrian
      Devonian

8. A. _____
   B. Triassic
      Silurian

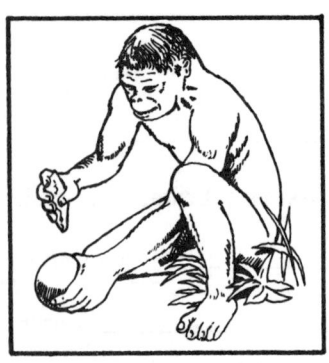   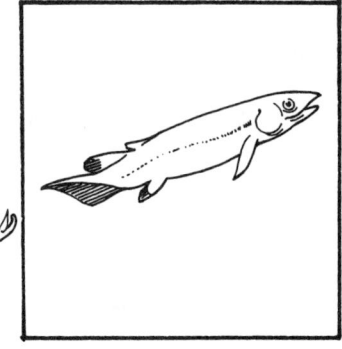

9. A. _____
   B. Tertiary
      Quaternary

10. A. _____
    B. Jurassic
       Tertiary

11. A. _____
    B. Jurassic
       Permian

12. A. _____
    B. Pre-Cambrian
       Pennsylvanian

11 Fossils and Prehistoric Life

A Last Look — Part III

A. Find the statement in the second column that best describes each word or group of words in the first column. Write the letter of the statement before the word it describes.

1. _____ cycad
2. _____ Brontosaurus
3. _____ *Homo sapiens*
4. _____ a meat-eating animal
5. _____ crinoid
6. _____ fossil
7. _____ Stegosaurus
8. _____ Pre-Cambrian
9. _____ a plant-eating animal
10. _____ Smilodon

a. stabbing cat
b. carnivore
c. earliest geological era
d. armored reptile
e. herbivore
f. today's man
g. thunder lizard
h. "sea lily," plant-like animal
i. evidence of ancient life
j. ancient palm-like tree

B. Circle the word or phrase that will make each sentence a true statement.

1. The first land plants appeared during the _____ period.

    Cambrian   Devonian   Permian

2. Land plants, such as scale trees, mosses and ferns, helped form the huge _____ deposits of today.

    coal   coral   mud

3. The Cenozoic Era is the _____ era in the geologic time scale.

    earliest   middle   latest

4. The vast forests of the Triassic period consisted of trees called _____.

    scale trees   spore trees   conifers

5. The _____ period is often called the "Age of Fishes."

    Cambrian   Devonian   Permian

6. Tyrannosaurus was a huge _____ reptile.

    carnivorous   herbivorous   amphibious

7. The Cenozoic Era is called the "Age of _____."

    Amphibians   Reptiles   Mammals

8. Most fossils were formed in _____.

    ice   water   trees

9. Prehistoric birds looked more like _____ than modern birds.

    plants   mammals   reptiles

10. Scientists divide units of time into eras, eras into periods, and periods into _____.

    epochs   calendars   scales

A Last Look — Part IV

A. Explain fully the meaning of this cartoon.

_____
_____
_____
_____

B. There is something wrong with each of these drawings. Circle the part of the picture that is incorrect and explain why you circled it.

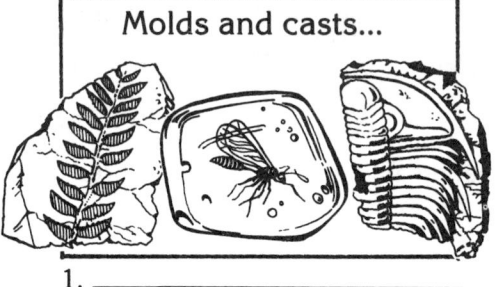

1. _____

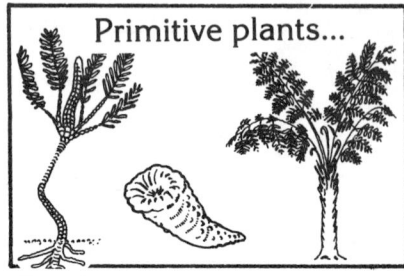

2. _____

Mesozoic Era...

3. _____

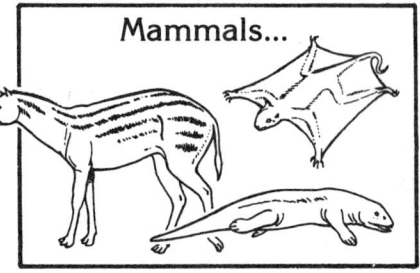

4. _____

C. Use these words to complete the puzzle below. When you have finished, the letters in the dark squares will spell a word that actually means "terrible lizards."

Pteranodon	Icthyosaurus	Dimetrodon
Triceratops	Stegosaurus	Hesperonis
Brontosaurus	Ankylosaurus	Tyrannosaurus

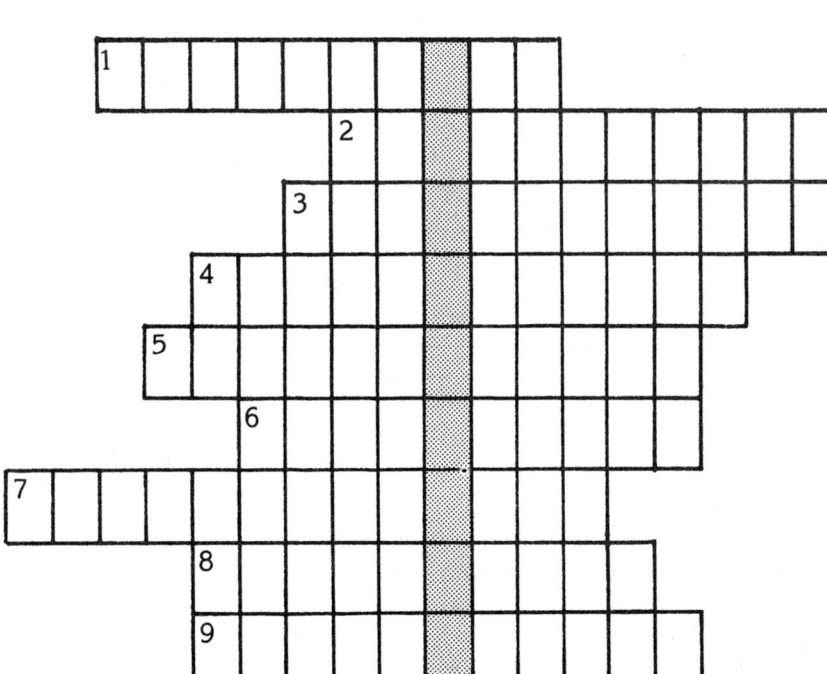

1. fin-back reptile
2. three-horned herbivore
3. the thunder lizard
4. heavily-armored herbivore
5. marine reptile
6. largest flying reptile
7. largest carnivore
8. a diving, flightless bird
9. had a double row of bony plates on its back

IV Fossils and Prehistoric Life

TRANSPARENCY SECTION

(Use the transparencies to introduce each lesson.)